FIRST POEMS

GEORGE CAMPBELL

FIRST POEMS

INTRODUCTION: KWAME DAWES

INTRODUCTORY POEM BY DEREK WALCOTT

PEEPAL TREE

First published by the author
in Kingston Jamaica in 1945
and reprinted with additional poems
by Garland Publishing Inc in 1981
This new edition published in 2012 by
Peepal Tree Press Ltd
17 King's Avenue
Leeds LS6 1QS
England

This edition restores the original sequence and layout of the 1945
edition but includes the additional poems in the 1981 edition as a
final section

ISBN13: 978 1 84523 1491

Supported by
ARTS COUNCIL
ENGLAND

To
Edna and Norman Manley Michael Manley
and
The People of Jamaica

GEORGE CAMPBELL

Read these poems with the simplicity of a leaf
receiving rain. The thick warm rain
of the Jamaican mountains, as strange
to your origins and as different from the blue
he writes, when he writes the word 'blue',
in 'In your clothing blue,
wrapping round you,
in the deep gloom
of an autumn room',
meaning an indigo with the scent of coffee
and the orange tang of pimento.
It is the way Lawrence tried to write like water,
or Whitman tried to write like the wind.
And reading them I am carried back over thirty years
to the cold green pastures and the stunted pine-trees
of mountain Jamaica of strawberries and conifers
and the springs that fell as clearly
as an iron hymn under a wooden chapel
over bridges and green gullies with dark rocks
above Gordon Town, still as a Sunday market
with the higglers' benches empty.
That's when the word revolution rang
like a single bell. Most of it's there,
but one has not been there so many years,
and something has yellowed in that light.
You take his Lenin. A figure on a poster,
but for Campbell then, Lenin was like Christ,
and maybe it is better to believe His Lenin
than to doubt Christ. There is an innocence
no politics can betray. And in this book
the best poems smell of that mountain wind,
the small good ones smell fresh as broken fruit,
and a few phrases still turn in the light like leaves.
The propagandist ones are curios,
like ochre posters for The People's Theatre,

the feverish elation of the first communes.
This hand was the first to stroke the beauty of ebony,
'Last Queries' turns round slowly on its pivot
like a peasant artifact, an artless sculpture,
without Mayakovsky's hysterical exultations
or that Laurential conceit. They are for the most part
purely without the egotism of personal pain,
and, at their nut is a grace
that has gone out of such directness.
Which of us would write now
such direct hymns of praise, litanies, benedictions
like 'Holy Be The White Head Of A Negro',
Or 'When I Pray', or Thomas Hart Benton's greeking
of a benign, pastoral South.
If the revolution has frozen to bas-relief postures,
and if from the clay there emerges
the flared nostrils of anger, in a wild stallion,
in a boxer, in the head of a Robeson,
behind it there was an attempt at a clear style
plain as Blake's forehead,
to be the first West Indian talking to people,
not to the distant roar of an electorate
since Claude MacKay had gone into exile,
while others composed black Parnassian.
When his worst rhetoric is washed away
what remains is Campbell, the love poet,
his love poems hurt as the best should
not with particular but with universal pain.
Even his love of people. They are like candles
on a windy verandah on a mountain night
that lean and straighten to your bending breath
on the clean page, they lean, and straighten,
but do not go out.
It is a good thing to have them again.

DEREK WALCOTT
Petit Valley Trinidad. April 1980

CONTENTS

POEMS FROM THE 1981 EDITION

INTRODUCTION

KWAME DAWES

The challenge of reading Jamaican poetry may lie, perhaps, in the absence of an accepted, even if flawed, narrative of its progression. Such narratives tend to imply the existence of a core of writers with a significant enough body of work to allow for some discussion of trends and directions.

As with much of English-speaking Caribbean poetry, prior to the early 1990s, the absence of a consistent venue for the publication of poetry from Jamaica, and, perhaps, the absence of writers with enough devotion to the business of publishing volumes of poetry, has meant that this kind of narrative has been hard to construct.

On paper, there is a through line of poetic production that might suggest that an aesthetic pattern could be constructed around what has been published. Unfortunately, even as someone who is the product of an education from the Caribbean, indeed an education focused on the study of Caribbean writing, I am faced with the simple fact that no such narrative was ever taught to me, nor have I been able to apply such an aesthetic framework to my understanding of Jamaican poetry. Instead, we have broad strokes: Claude McKay's dialect poems,[1] a cluster of heavily colonial writers still stuck in the imitative patterns of Georgian verse,[2] a spate of scattered but inconsistent poetic production fired by the nationalism of the late 1930s that includes George Campbell,[3] another scattering of pre-independence voices,[4] and then the march of names becomes more distinctive: Mervyn Morris, Dennis Scott, Edward Baugh, Tony McNeill, Lorna Goodison, Olive Senior, and so on.

Except for the writers named above, others who might be slotted into these broad categories can only be found in the various anthologies and sporadic editions of *Focus* that tried to make the case for a Jamaican poetry movement every ten or fifteen years.

So while we knew individual poems by poets like H.D. Carberry, Una Marson, M.G. Smith, Roger Mais, Neville Dawes and so on, we couldn't speak of truly having an understanding of their poetic aesthetics, styles or thematic interests in the way that one might be able to speak of Morris, Goodison or McNeill. The reason: too few books, too few copies, too rapid disappearance. (Thankfully, this dispersal of evidence has started to be reversed in recent years, with the publication of collections of Carberry, M.G. Smith, Una Marson and Neville Dawes.[5])

During the pre-independence period, the situation was the same throughout the West Indies – that is, few books and generally a sense of Caribbean poetry in English being defined by the work that appeared in *Bim*, *Focus*, *Kyk-over-al* and the *Caribbean Voices* programme on the BBC. In a series of short essays written in the early 1950s, for instance, a young recent Oxford graduate, Neville Dawes, was being very consciously pioneering in attempting to speak about the nature of West Indian poetry – its aesthetic shape and its preoccupations.

"Prolegomenon to the Poetry of the West Indies" eventually found its way into a brief, pamphlet publication from the Extra Mural Department at the University of the West Indies.[6] This 1950s study is a valiant effort, but what is quickly apparent is that Dawes is searching for patterns in what is a thin body of work. Derek Walcott, who at the time had three self-published chapbooks of poems[7] – a poet who is barely into his twenties, that is – becomes the senior poet, the standing example of a modern Caribbean poetry.

To appreciate the dilemma, one only need compare the situation with poetry to the situation with fiction. At the time of Dawes' efforts, there already existed novels by de Lisser, Lamming, Mendes, Mittelholzer, McKay, Reid, Rhys, C.L.R. James, Mais, Selvon and many more. Over the next ten years the situation for poetry remained fairly unchanged, while the list of novels and short story collections grew so dramatically that we often referred to this period as a kind of golden age of West Indian writing. For poetry, it was really only the emergence of Brathwaite, Carter and Walcott as published poets that marked a significant change. Trinidad had one major voice, Eric Roach, but no collection of his poems became available until 1992. Moreover, the kind of mapping of Jamaican/Caribbean poetry that Neville Dawes began, and that I would have found useful as an undergraduate, did not begin to appear until Lloyd W. Brown's *West Indian Poetry* (1984), J. Edward Chamberlin's *Come Back to Me My Language* (1993) and Laurence Breiner's *Introduction to Caribbean Poetry* (1998).

I offer this lengthy preliminary as what I believe is a necessary context for introducing George Campbell's *First Poems*. Here is the thing: *First Poems* existed as a collection during this time of critical silence. Campbell had published the first edition of the book himself in 1945. He was the poster child of the Edna Manley movement of discovery. She is said to have discovered him when he was a teenager and helped orchestrate the publication of the poems.[8] He was adopted by the Manleys and quoted greatly, celebrated as the Poet of Revolution. Yet, in all my studies of Caribbean literature, I never studied the poetry of Campbell. I read a few selections in anthologies, but that was it. I never had to contend with a full body of work. Campbell, therefore, was known to me as an icon – a valiant voice determined to write poetry rooted in Jamaican experience, a new voice breaking away from the past, a gifted writer who, given other circumstances and a different time, might have come to be quite a giant in Caribbean poetry. His work, however, particularly in its first 1945 incarnation, was given very little detailed attention, and I have seen only two significant assessments in response to the republication of *First Poems* in 1981. These were Derek Walcott's poem introducing the 1981 volume, and a review of that volume by Neville Dawes in the *Gleaner* in that year.[9] These pieces, in their brief, suggestive ways, begin the process of sifting a Campbell for the 1980s.

Both Walcott and Dawes record a debt, admit what has been

bypassed by time, and settle on a fairly similar estimation of what still lives in Campbell's poetry.

The debt for both is in the escape from, in Walcott's phrase, "Black Parnassus", and Neville Dawes' feeling that after the poems of 1945 were published, "We were then certain that we no longer needed to write poetry over the Victorian grid with 'Pan' still sleeping in the brake." For Dawes, Campbell is "Jamaica's first modernist poet". For both, he is also the herald of the long-delayed revolution to overthrow the old Caribbean racial hierarchies: for Walcott, "This hand was the first to stroke the beauty of ebony"; for Dawes, "the first poet of the nationalist movement that had to begin by looking at Black people, but always remembered 'blue eyes/Dark hands/Red hair'".[10] For both Walcott and Dawes, by the 1980s, Campbell's focus on race was a necessary but historic achievement.

Both agree on the Campbell that had weathered less well: the political poems that Walcott describes as "curios,/like ochre posters for The People's Theatre". Neville Dawes, lifelong Marxist, is even less forgiving of the Campbell who wrote "Christ kissed Lenin on the lips", dismissing it as "simply bizarre... an adolescent dream". A stern critic of bourgeois nationalism, Neville Dawes wonders "in real puzzlement, just what 'revolution' N.W. Manley thought that Campbell was poet of". Yet, as Walcott writes, there was a revolution, but it was in poetry not politics.

For Dawes this poetic revolution came from Campbell showing "that it was possible to maintain sound by using rhymes in the manner of cement [I think he means this just in the sense of something that joins] rather than steel locks. The pure pieces are like music pure and fine." For both it is the lyric Campbell that "has never died"; the poems, in Walcott's words, that "attempt at a clear style/ plain as Blake's forehead" or, for Dawes, "delicate" poems such as "Drought".

But unstinting as both are in their praise of the best writing, Walcott's poem throws out a challenge to us as twenty-first century readers that we have to decide whether we can meet. In a neat ambiguity of grammar he instructs us to "Read these poems with the simplicity of a leaf/receiving rain" and admits, "at their nut is a grace/ that has gone out of such directness./Which of us would write now/ Such direct hymns of praise…?" How then do we approach George Campbell's poetry after another thirty years of historically induced cynicism and self-reflexive sophistication?

*

The reissue of this collection of poems tells us that while we can't fully rescue Campbell from the kind of obscurity that comes with a small body of work, we can at least begin to engage with his work as a critical part of the larger narrative of Jamaican writing, and as worthy in its own right of examination and rediscovery.

What is hard to deny, however, is why Campbell remained not much more than an iconic figure, iconic in the way that some occasional poets might be, and for us more distantly historic. Some of his classic work remains heavily anthologised in the way that Langston Hughes, for instance, is anthologised. But compared to Hughes, Campbell's output is slim. And while a slim body of work does not imply the absence of value, what is striking about Campbell is that his work does not really span his lifetime as one understands the relatively small output of, say, Gerard Manley Hopkins did. Campbell, essentially, remained a poet of 1945 – a poet for the moment (though some of the later poems show no slackening of the lyric gift). Yet because he wrote those poems at such a pivotal moment in Jamaican and Caribbean literary history, his moment offers a fit prism through which to view the poetry produced by Caribbean poets after him.

As a poet, George Campbell appears to straddle two impulses that reveal that he was as much a poet shaped by the poetics of the late nineteenth century and early twentieth century as he was by the modernist trends of the 1930s and 1940s. At times the verse seems shaped and heavily influenced by the conventions of nature worship that we have come to associate with the Romantic poets. Here the landscape overwhelms the poet; he almost weeps as he cries out, "God, I love this place!" in reference to St Ann. What makes these expressions compelling, however, is that they come from a poet living in a colonised world who is expressing a certain kind of primordial nationalism, the kind that allows him to distinguish himself from the colonial imagination both in his conception of self and his conception of the landscape. And love for the natal landscape, as George Lamming reminds us,[11] is the deepest, truest touchstone of the national instinct. Colonial verse often seems apologetic in finding local analogues for Shelley's skylark, but George Campbell displays an unquestioning confidence in the idea of finding poetic possibility in the specifics of his own landscape – his island landscape. He refers to the flora – the yellow cassia flowers, the green cacti, the scarlet poinsettia – in the poem "Litany" in which daylight is "like a sacrament in my hands/ Amen". We see this attitude of worship throughout the poems, even when nature is not what is holding his attention.

Campbell complicates this adoration of the landscape with a common trope – the landscape as stand-in for a lover. So many of the poems in here are unabashed love songs, and the love is never free of angst and loss.

> The night is naked
> And it wears no clothes
> No shadow moonlight
> To distort the night
> The night is naked
> And it wears no clothes
>
> Black is the night's hair
> Black is the night's face
> No moon
> No stars… ("The Night", p. 43, this edition)

Campbell uses the landscape to speak of the sexuality of his lovers, and in doing so, he begins to achieve the second critical part of his contribution to the poetics of the Caribbean: at the heart of this merging of the landscape and the body of his lover is the adoration of the body of, first, the black woman, and then, by explicit extension, the black body:

Your blackness steeps through me
It wets like dew
It comes upon me like a lovely night.
You are not here
Your blackness stays round me like rich perfume
All space black dew.
Your absence beautiful against my loins
Oh! lovely woman like a velvet night! (#31, p. 71)

Campbell's 1938 poems reveal a clear debt to the poetry of Langston Hughes and the Negritude poets of the 1920s and 30s. He is determined to celebrate blackness as beautiful. His poem "Holy" is often quoted as the poem that begins to express the beauty and dignity in the black body, and there is a certain quality here that speaks to the generosity of his feelings, but I suspect that the appeal of this poem is also its conservatism – its ecumenical possibilities – because at its heart, while it does claim the beauty of the black body, "Holy be the white head of a Negro./ Sacred be the black flax of a black child" (p. 69), it is careful to speak of the beauty of all races and colours. We find this pattern in other poems by Campbell ("Let Us Build"), but even the more compelling and forceful poems that unabashedly speak to the beauty of the black body are never straightforward. They are troubling and they present the dilemma of race in moving ways. In "Last Queries" the speaker asks, "So, is my skin beautiful?" The poem begins there, and then takes itself along the journey of a black community's life, constantly asking whether there is beauty in the rituals of the black experience. The question is rhetorical, but it is edged with a dare, a kind of challenge that we should not be surprised by in Campbell's work.

Campbell is able to take us through the questions of the black body into increasingly political territory, territory that begins with the famous poem, "Negro Aroused", which is an unapologetic shout of protest, resistance and threat, that speaks of the enslavement and abuse of the black body and the black person, and the extent to which such abuse can cause shame in the black person. In his anthem to the body of the black woman, he describes coming upon a naked woman with her child in arms in a river ("Mother", p. 72). He is struck by her beauty; she, surprised, tries to cover herself; he appeals to her to show herself, to not be ashamed and she "laughs to show her glory".

But Campbell does not ignore the fact that the woman's body works hard. In his poems, he is deeply sympathetic to the hardships that the black woman must endure as a worker. She is a stone-breaker, she bears her children, she farms, she endures, but what stands out always is his quest to find in these things a certain beauty, a dignity that can be celebrated.

Campbell's more political poems include pieces that were often invoked by the Manleys during their political campaigns. Poems like "Democracy" could easily be labelled what Walcott terms "yellowed" propaganda:

> If from this blackness
> New flowers shall rise
> If out of the darkness
> We focus our eyes
> Towards a destiny
> Towards a nation
> Of democracy.
> Not now leaderless
> With this elation
> Work now untireless
> Towards this building
> Of Socialism. (p. 105)

What is striking about these political poems is that for Campbell the rise of democracy and political independence is deeply rooted in a racial dynamic. There is, though, no acknowledgment in these poems that Manley – the leader – is hardly a part of the black masses that he is leading.

This is why I think in Campbell's poem "On this Night" something quite curious happens. The poem, he notes, was written on the occasion of the formation of the People's National Party in 1938, yet one has the sense that it was not simply written "on the occasion", but specifically for Norman Manley – a poem that could have formed part of a speech, even if he did not actually declaim it. The speaker assumes the position of a leader of the people, and appears to be speaking in the voice of the educated bourgeoisie that is coming to lead the poor and the workers out of their misery. It is a poem which expresses much the same ideological thrust as V.S. Reid's novel *New Day* (1949), one that puts the tumultuous black masses under the firm control of the educated (and often brown) middle class. It has a prosaic tone and the rhetorical posture is patronising, a position that we don't see much of in Campbell's work, but it appears to show us the extent to which, as a young man, he was taken with the leadership of Manley and his movement. I say "appears" to show Campbell's tutelage to the Manleys, but in the context of so much that rings absolutely true in Campbell's work, is it possible that the patronising voice contains a note of irony?:

> Or are there hard words in the dark: are you
> Formless dust blown in the wind?
> Bullets answered your gesture for wages
> Sometime back; we give no cause for bullets
> We shall lead you to a freedom that will
> Elevate you from bullets. Shall improve your
> Mind: only the stupid stumble in the
> Way of bullets.
> You are politically dormant; not
> Appreciating your democratic
> Institutions. Is it not right you should
> Know how to use your own weapons of rule? (p. 106)

In "New Constitution 1945", Campbell continues to write with the posture of the poet who must write for the occasion. The poets who do this best are those who manage to find a metaphor that somehow retains its sophistication while effectively conveying a truth with directness and simplicity. And here, in the legal metaphors of rental and land purchase, Campbell finds a truth that unites the position of a still colonised Jamaican people, both leadership and masses:

Now we turn tenants at will no longer
Spiritual heirs of God. Our spirit stronger
Let's now look to inheritance
Of our earth. With claim made stronger
By our achievements, our natural dignity.

This land will speak with voices
Of destiny. Voices from victory
Of ownership in proud estate. (p. 110)

One can't miss a deep pathos in the poem – a scrupulous resistance to any hint of celebration – indeed, there is a clipped, sardonic quality of irony which makes clear that what has been granted is hardly enough. Written, one presumes, in 1945, it is useful to remember that a couple of years prior, Roger Mais had been arrested and jailed for sedition for questioning whether colonised people should support their coloniser in a war that they, the colonised people, had no real stake in.

There are other themes that occupy Campbell. Death, for instance, recurs in many of his love poems and his more philosophical pieces. What is fairly obvious about these intimations of death is that they come from a place of youth – there is a self-consciousness about the fascination with death, not as a genuine threat but as an opponent to life. The poems about death are not poems about ageing or about dying, but are, instead, poems that ask the existential question of why we are here and what happens to us once we are no longer here. These are the intimations of youth, and at times they manage to achieve the sublime.

When Campbell combines his preoccupation with beauty, blackness and life, death seems to be only a temptation to put aside. In his version of Keats' "Ode on a Grecian Urn" (#33), Campbell sees in his urn a decidedly black figure. The poem is worth quoting in full. It is a sophisticated work that serves as a prototype for the kind of gestures that Derek Walcott would make throughout his career with increasing sophistication:

New-world Flowers
Spring-time Negroes
The land calling
Clean fresh showers
Of rain falling
The Grecian heroes
Even features;
These new creatures
With strong noses
Life exuberant
Mouth protuberant
Walking about the world today.

I love Spring-time
I love flowers
I love the freshness of the grass
One day I came upon a glass
Of Grecian make
I would not break

Classical glass
Far back in thought:
Define your needs
Look what I bought
A pack of seeds
To sprinkle all the world today. (p. 74)

The impulse not to break the classical glass, suggesting a reluctance to destroy the Grecian symbol of Western hegemony, is a fascinating one. Yet the speaker is not without agency. The speaker, an adorer of his landscape, of the flowers of spring, of the world where his Negro "Grecians" walk, carries with him the seed that he will sow in the new world. As the husbandman of the new landscape, he has now occupied it. Indeed, he has defined his needs and has proceeded to meet them. Yet at the same time, he wishes to locate his new poetic landscape in the terrain of high art, connecting, via Keats, to the classical past claimed by the West.

This is, at least, how I am tempted to read the poem. What is undeniable is that Campbell was grappling with the meaning of being a writer in a colonial landscape, and his poetic directions reflect that struggle, a struggle that produced work of importance.

Campbell, as Walcott and Neville Dawes made clear, gave other poets permission to begin to chart the full range of thoughts and feelings that surround being a Jamaican person, a Caribbean person. Even when some of his experiments can't be claimed to wholly work, they open up significant directions for others to explore. Poem #53, for instance, would serve as a perfect epigraph for novels like Mais's *The Hills Were Joyful Together*, Patterson's *The Children of Sisyphus* and the film *The Harder They Come* by Perry Henzell:

> In the slums
> Jewel staring eyes
> Of human flies
> Crowd the rims
> Of our social order.
> We avoid
> The stench of slums
> Everything uncomfortable
> Insistence
> Of staring eyes
> Evidence
> Of substanceless limbs.
>
> Here are –
> Bilious houses
> At the womb-head
> Of comfort
> Riches
> Pleasure.
>
> Here are –
> Magnificent skeletons
> With shrinking skins

> Shrinking
> With our approval
> Here is
> The world we accept
> From our glass houses. (p. 102)

The poet is outside of the world he is describing, and he honestly positions himself in the world of the middle class. The complications of this task of speaking for the poor and yet speaking from a position of relative privilege is one that will consume so many of the writers who followed Campbell. What he achieves here is a willingness to confront a Jamaican world that is not thick with the tourist clichés of beauty and paradise.

Campbell does have limitations as a poet, even as he attempts to do things that will become increasingly important in Jamaican poetry. In this collection there is, for example, one dialect poem. Its halting meter and garbled syntax are not a reflection of the quality of patois language at the time, but an indication of just how difficult it was for a poet like Campbell to capture dialect in verse. His poem appeared long after McKay's *Constab Ballads* of 1912, and around the time when Louise Bennett was beginning what would become her legendary career as a writer and performer of dialect poetry.[10] Their facility with creole language far exceeded Campbell's.

He is far more accomplished when he does not attempt to recreate the dialect, when he relies instead on the form of the folk song as a basis for a poem, building on its beautifully elliptical and rhythmical qualities, more rhythmically interesting, indeed, than much of his work. In "Folk Poem" there is a wonderful mastery when he allows the folk meter to guide him. The effect is fetching:

> Play
> Moon shine baby
> Moon shine baby
> Sing out children
>
> June, giddy, newly born

Shining silver eyes so bright
Spread out in the moon pool;
Moon baby,
Moon baby –
Broken shining plates around her
Gold and blue flakes surround her.

Moon shine baby
Moon shine dolly.

"O stop that" –
Mother cries,
"Mind my baby
Mind my dolly
Mind her eyes!" (p. 94)

It is, however, in a poem such as "Emancipation", one of Campbell's longest works, that we see his great value as a poet of public statement and authority (as well as more private lyric grace). Campbell is a politician's dream because he offers lines so quotable and so carefully constructed that they are irresistible. Campbell wrote for his time and wrote at a time when the voice needed was the voice that worked through the uncertainties of the movement towards independence, and yet managed to offer a confident rhetorical basis for it. In "Emancipation" Campbell argues that the act of resistance and rebellion is endemic to Jamaican society, not as a point of shame and concern, but as a point of pride. He argues that these acts were necessary and indications of the truest civility of those who stood up and resisted:

Here in Jamaica
Memorial lights in our living,
Revolt every five years
In one hundred and fifty years
Twenty-nine revolts in Annunciation
Of freedom, the Annunciation of the Spirit. (p. 148)

In this poem, Campbell shows the extent to which his poetics relies both on the language of the King James Bible and on overturning the core constructs of that bible, at least as they had been appropriated and employed by the coloniser:

> Know there is no disgrace to be cast into bond life
> And hate bondage
> Know there is no disgrace to be born into bond life
> And seek new life (p. 147)

In this poem he describes the resistance from slavery and emancipation as the great resurrection, the true resurrection, and he creates a most quotable line of deep resistance that would be fleshed out by the reggae artists of the 1970s as an active and necessary act: "And questing death is the final mockery of the oppressors". This is no doubt the kind of poem in which Walcott hears the parallels with D.H. Lawrence (who "tried to write like water") or Walt Whitman (who "tried to write like the wind").

Campbell names three heroes, Sam Sharpe, Cudjoe and William Knibb. Until the 1960s and 70s, these names were not commonplace at all. He describes them as "forgotten heroes", and in his poem he seeks to "resurrect" them and give them presence and voice.

No doubt, Campbell's poetry will continue to be read in public places and on public occasions well into the future, as long as his work is available to be spoken. There is much about his language, sometimes so steeped in nineteenth century idiom and diction that it appears to belong to a different time than the modernist world in which he was writing. But this is a language that we see becoming a part of the post-independence idiom of Jamaican society – the transformed biblical language of the Rastaman. Campbell was still working out the path to his own idiom, his own Jamaican voice, and in the process offered at least one act of liberation: the eschewing of the rigid rhyme scheme and the metrical line for something more fluid, something akin to the language of Whitman, and a voice, as it turns out, affirmed by the modernist movement of the time of his most prolific production.

It may, though, be an irony of Campbell's reputation that it might endure less in the poems he is best known for, and more in his quieter, unremarked work, such as "The Road" (1955). This certainly was the conclusion Wayne Brown came to in an obituary notice on Campbell's death in 2002.[11] Here rhythm, parallels, patterns of sound and a visual sense of proportion cohere in the most lucid way:

> We must carve ourselves
> From the confusion of a selfish world
> A road of flashing faith
> And calm good sense
> A road that will glance
> Like a miracle […]
> Through all atomic clouds
> To a way of life:
> Such as a man's way with a woman,
> Such as fertile earth with an ear of corn,
> Such as truth with reason,
> Such as flowering in season
> When a collective people breathes good will
> Because they mean good and are one at heart…
>
> (p. 155)

His ability to speak to other eras and other poets concerned with making it new is revealed in a poem by Jamaica's most thoroughgoing modernist, Anthony McNeill, which very recently came to my attention, from his as yet unpublished collection, *Choruses in the Summer of Clear*.[12] The poem, given in full at the end of this introduction (pp. 31-32), makes clear (beyond the unresisted temptation to cheek a poetic father) just how much of a ladder to heaven Campbell's poetry offered.

There is little question that if any poet can be rightly described as a Caribbean classic, it is Campbell. He articulated what many of his contemporaries and those coming after him hoped to do. He offered a poetics rooted in race, in identity, in a certain kind of nationalism and in a political ideology that was taking root in the region –

Socialism. It is likely, as I have suggested, that what will endure will be those poems that reveal a deep reflection into the meaning of his identity and his place in the world around him. Those restrained, pellucid poems, marked by uncertainty and hope, are the lasting legacy of George Campbell.

End Notes

1. See Claude McKay, *Songs of Jamaica* (London: Gardner, 1912) and *Constab Ballads* (London: Watts, 1912).

2. The Parnassians (alias the Jamaican Poetry League, founded 1923) were led by a black Jamaican, J.E.C. McFarlane, author of *Daphne* and *Selected Shorter Poems* (Kingston: The Pioneer Press, 1954) and its belated manifesto *A Literature in the Making* (Kingston: The Pioneer Press,1956). The League published an anthology, *Voices from Summerland* (1929). Leading members included Constance Hollar, Lena Kent and Albinia Hutton. McFarlane wrote of growing up in "another kind of world, a world which had some appreciation of universal values", by which he meant a mix of imperial cultural values and denial of the reality of race in Jamaican society.

3. These are the poets whose work is to be found in *Focus* (1943, 1948, 1960), such as Vera Bell, H.D. Carberry, M.G. Smith, Roger Mais, George Campbell.

4. For instance, A.L. Hendriks, Basil McFarlane, R.L.C. McFarlane and John Figueroa.

5. See H.D. Carberry, *It Takes a Mighty Fire* (Kingston: Ian Randle Publishers, 1995); M.G. Smith, In the Kingdom of Light (Kingston: The Mill Press, 2004); Una Marson, *Selected Poems* (Leeds: Peepal Tree Press, Caribbean Modern Classics, 2010) and Neville Dawes, *Fugue and Other Writings* (Leeds: Peepal Tree, 2012).

6. I haven't been able to trace my printed copy of the original "Prolegomena to the Poetry of the West Indies", a very different work to the pamphlet published as *Prolegomena to Caribbean*

Literature (Kingston: Institute of Jamaica for the African Caribbean, 1977). Reprinted in *Fugue and Other Writings*.

7. These were *25 Poems* (Port of Spain: Guardian Commercial Printery, 1948 and Bridgetown: Advocate, 1949); *Epitaph for the Young* (Bridgetown: Advocate, 1949) and *Poems* (Kingston: City Printery, 1951).

8. *First Poems* was privately published in Kingston in 1945; it was reprinted with additional poems and in a revised order in 1981, with Walcott's poem (see pp. 6-7), by Garland Publishing Inc., New York.

9. *Sunday Gleaner*, 29 November 1981.

10. Neville Dawes referenced the classic "Negro Aroused", "I Was Negro" and "Holy", amongst others.

11. See George Lamming, *Of Age and Innocence* (Leeds: Peepal Tree Press, Caribbean Modern Classics edition, 2011; first published in 1958), p. 185, on the "silent and sacred communion".

12. Louise Bennett's three earliest publications appeared before the publication of Campbell's *First Poems*. They were: *Dialect Verses* (Kingston: Herald, 1942); *Jamaican Humour in Dialect* (Kingston: Jamaica Press Association, 1943) and *Anancy Stories and Poems in Dialect* (Kingston: Gleaner, 1944).

13. "Do I Live Here?", *Jamaica Sunday Gleaner*, November 24 2002.

14. Peepal Tree Press is working on producing a collected edition of McNeill's work, of which *Choruses in the Summer of Clear* is a small part.

Anthony McNeill
from *Choruses in the Summer of Clear* (written c. 1976)

Ulysses is the noise it discesses
meant to say -cusses

the wind blew right at the end
so the flower

said yes
the mirror reversin:g

god mouth

———————

the air
the bell
the blue

flower
george camp-
bell   ladder

to heaven
ladder out

ta de long ache
ladder in to

the light   the dark
gate of such light

as the poles
in repris-

ing kept
the same form

so I say to him
camp   bell

say to him geor-
gie   pud-

ding and pie
a poem begins

the nursery rhymes
as the name in the barn

falls on itself
missing the ghost

walking through it
poem be ghost through

the last ache   poem be name
on the ultimate bell

poem be leaf on the penitent face
poem be honest and true in the lull

FIRST POEMS

RELEASE

Let my dreams hang intact round my tree
And let my branches reach in every land,
So all the peoples of the world might see
The beauty and the tear-drops from my hands.
Let there be loftiness
And sun-lit sky
And over all blue unity of space
And there be world possession of my trunk,
Spread thus my dreams.

TREES

But this night is momentous:
You and I trees planted far apart
Trying to touch one another. You trying
To understand, and I the wind pleading through
My leaves; what keeps the distance?
And mark, you have been planted centuries
Before me, and are strong. While I so
Sudden in your life surviving the strength
That vanquished others, and now worried to death
How peacefully to whisper under your shade
Embracing your leaves and mine – to win together.

Both of us are dreaming of the splendid dawn,
Are you going to leave me and forge ahead
Alone? Both of us have splendid dreams
Splendid fruit may come, are you going to eat
Alone, not say to me come on?
Both of us are feeling what the end will mean,
I wonder if you'll say to me come and win
With us?
The western sky is flaming with the dying sun
The splendid daylight feels the night creep down.
I wonder why those stars come up at such
Grand distances: Like brilliant unfriendly Beings
Standing alone
The stars shine at their brightest, Dawn is coming fast
I wonder if these splendid ones will say come
On with us?

1937

We went out into the moonlight last night,
Into rich liquid, suffusing every
Thing; untouchable, intangible, it
Drank in our bodies; there was completeness
Fuller than man's contact with woman
Oneness completer than upon a horse.
We climbed the wet hill into the flush that,
Surrounding us, caressing, kissing us,
Swept us from ourselves, and we slid to find
The world an orange mellowness, just like
      golden twilight.
Then we sat on the barbecues and looked
Down grade on ghost like moonlight through the
Guava trees; like an aged orchard, as if
Time with its memories, peace, forgetfulness
Had stopped, was still in its graveyard around
The hazy guava trees.
O moonlight, face of time, completeness, we
Were eternal, unearthy and part of God.

St. Ann, September 1938

I could kiss this place
This rich scenery
And press it close like a woman to me.
I know that these green hills only can be
Mistress passionless.
Grass inanimate
All this greenery
Surrounding me.
These round and low green hills dotted with trees
No sound but my sighing and the humming breeze.
How I love this place
Exquisite distress
Inarticulate.
Oh what moves so deep as in bed at night
Tide restless sleep sigh out both joy and fright.
Scene excitable
Inexplicable
Unexplainable.
God I love this place!

St. Ann

- 6 -

I have done wrong
I have destroyed a glass I cannot mend.
I have crushed life.
True that the glass was once cracked already
But it was whole.
Tonight a current will run through these hands
The whole idea of time and space will go.
They are taking
What they can't give back
But I did wrong.

ESSENTIAL

And if they see my heart
Will they see the music that
Flows through me
Bringing songs to my hands
And will they see the flame
Which is my being and my will?

O have I opened my heart
Beyond all opening
The essential being
Within me
Unfound
Unknown.

I WILL COME

In your clothing blue,
Wrapping round you,
In the sweet gloom
Of an autumn room,
I will come,
I will find you,
I will know you,
Everyday.

Who's that riding to Patmos,
Riding across the Bay?

In your blue world
Of nothingness
I will come,
I will possess you,
Everyday.

THE NIGHT

The night is naked
And it wears no clothes
No shadow moonlight
To distort the night
The night is naked
And it wears no clothes.

Black is the night's hair
Black is the night's face
No moon
No stars
The night is naked
And it wears no stars.

LITANY

I hold the splendid daylight in my hands
Inwardly grateful for a lovely day.
Thank you life.
Daylight like a fine fan spread from my hands
Daylight like scarlet poinsettia
Daylight like yellow cassia flowers
Daylight like clean water
Daylight like green cacti
Daylight like sea sparkling with white horses
Daylight like sunstrained blue sky
Daylight like tropic hills
Daylight like a sacrament in my hands.
Amen.

Above the sea
Peace in the lofty hills
Birds sing with me
My inspiration is in love with me.

Give me the Dawn
Give me your promise, Dawn,
Winds sing with me
My inspiration is in love with me.

Fashion a necklace of words
Sunlight of words in your breast
When you are weary of words
Remembrest
Dawnlight of words in the skies
Did their share
Sunlight and dew for the trees.

Diamonds of words from your hair
Sparkles of words from your eyes
Why weepest?
Music of words in the breeze
Grainlights the sands for the seas.

Listen, Moon,
Last night you died too soon
I looked for you
And you had fled
The world was dead
And residue of nothingness
In my head.
Listen, Moon,
Last night you died too soon
I held my lover in my arms
And you were dead
And you were dead
I will never see her face again.
I will never see her face again.

— 14 —

FLAMING DIRECTIONS

Oh if some of the flaming directions will live,
And time be not only for here,
If death is only a portal to give,
Some new phase anywhere,
If only the hairs on a man's hand and his skin,
Are the things that end
And there be some detached design for the mind to blend.

O crying pain, oh sea of hurt onward,
I cannot bow to you, Death,
Only those unfound, revoked,
Must bow to you.

Who escapes?
Is time alone for her and this the end-all?
Oh! but some of these flaming directions will live,
In purpose continual!

II

Meeting you is
Opening my window into bursting day
When night comes
Why should I weep?
Leaving you is
Knowing in me deep
Flowers of you.

When we part

     'Twill be night for me
There'll be no songs left.

     All lights out
     'Twill be dark.

Where we part
There'll be no world left.

MY LOVE

My love a crucifix to place
Within Time's hands.
I die, my love still has its place
Upon Time's wall.
Every act, every dream,
Every presence
Time cages.
So lives my love
So lives your body
So lives my utter want.
Time will never end.
Lovers will whisper o'er
My love, a crucifix of dust
Upon Time's breast.

Now I feel the full torture of love
Now I know there's a tremendous lover inside me
Crushing, hurting, making
Day and night alike
For I awake from sleep and feel the pain of my love,
And because there can be no fulfilment,
I must keep
This demon this torture inside me,
What other lover can I find
Will there be any respite?
Because this love it hurts too much
And tortures too terribly.

We have visited strange places of pain in our minds
We have touched the end of things
And have reached final termini.
The moments have stripped all leaves and left us naked
And stark
Bare like the stars
Wombless like stone.
Let us return from the riverside
You and I
Having found the door of release
Having known the beginning and end into continuum
Let us look into each other's eyes
Into the great face of silence
And understand.

— 20 —

MY BITTER JOY

My bitter joy when you are near
Wound always there
Wound always bare
Time never heals
Death only ends
Time only seals
What life suspends.

DROUGHT

No love in my heart
No love in my tree
And I can go down to the sea
And weep my tears
No laughter in my eyes
No laughter in my mouth
And all the land is gold and dry
Thirsting in drought.

MAGDALENE

It was his serenity
Brought me sanity.
There was no lust in his eyes
No look of surprise
At my naked flesh
No willingness
To be caught in the mesh
Of the loveliness
That had bored my ears.

I felt secure
As I knelt at his feet
And had no fears
That at dead of night
I would hear the beat
In an outside room,
Creak of a door
And demand of my womb.

It was his serenity
That held me so
I would not go
Away from the side
Of man enticed
His passions denied
For his way of life.

In memory
Of moments
Circled
No final flames
Or soot
The end of days.
In memory
Of the continual
Ended.
Green finished days
Salute!

III

NEGRO AROUSED

Negro aroused! Awakened from
The ignominious sleep of dominance!
Freedom! off with these shackles
That torment, I lift my head and scream to heaven
Freedom! Now my body is strong, strong!
Now the blood rushes through my veins
And boils up in my head at their insult.
The spirit of freedom is resurrected in me,
I lift my head and cry to heaven defiance,
Freedom! Let them beat down this house,
Muscle built, stifle this screaming voice,
Let them! We are aroused! Fear made us shut our eyes
Once; made us give up Freedom to save our flesh
But my eyes now flash to the very heavens defiance; and
My skin is hard; lash it, O world, and
Bring your battering-rams of insults and discomforts
You that hate others to live! We are no longer
Stampeding cattle. No! The hot fire of new blood
Bubbles under this skin; the heart shouts Freedom!
I lift my face to heaven, awakened, shouting louder, louder
With triumph, with a new found strength –
Freedom! We cry only freedom – we were dead when
Sleeping – now we live! live! We are aroused!

LAST QUERIES

Say, is my skin beautiful? —
Soft as velvet,
As deep as the blackness of a weeping night.
And my teeth? —
Like ivory tusks,
As white as the sea foam that catches light.
Say, is my hair beautiful? —
As a bear's coat,
As bright as chips of black marble found in oil.
And my muscles? —
Like a tiger's back,
You are as pleasing as of wet rich soil.
Say, are my eyes beautiful? —
Like wet marble,
As valuable as pearls in oysters found at sea.
And my mind? —
Like bright sunlight,
Wonderful you would be if you were free!
Say, is my voice beautiful? —
Really beautiful?
As fine a music as ever cheered us here,
And my strength? —
Durable as iron,
It's a pity to be with such despair.

Say, are my sacrifices beautiful? —
Like a mother's,
As noble as the martyrdom of a saint.
And my love? —
Like unto woman's
Say, are my features beautiful? —
As a great mountain's
As strong as the ruggedness that grace the poor.
And my hope? —

Like a discoverer's
Alas! that we will never open wide our door!
Could my death be beautiful? –
Like a fallen rose
As quietly as a gentle wind dies at sea.
In death could I be beautiful? –
Like wet black marble
Oh misery! poor youth and the world needs thee.

I was Negro: mechanical beast of burden.
These knotted arms and muscled back
Have borne loads that my very soul felt,
And I have struggled on too proud
To give in. But now, Oh My God,
I feel tired   ...   tired!

I was Negro: mechanical beast of burden.
These cut up rough hands so black
Have made goads that were my own belt,
And I could have screamed aloud
To heaven. But now, Oh My God,
I feel tired   ...   tired!

I was Negro: mechanical beast of burden.
But now –
I could stamp down a world mountain
On my own body and shut out
The sky, the sea, and everything
I scream: I am tired   ...   tired!

I was Negro: mechanical beast of burden.
But now –
I could burn up this breast of a christian,
For in no other life could I take the load,
Nor look for peace.
My God! I am tired   ...   tired!

I scorn the lot of the rich man,
Like a convict I shun the road,
And this man must cease!
I was Negro: mechanical beast of burden,
But now I am tired!

MOTHER AT BED OF HER DYING SON

Oh! how my eyes are wet
Although you go to rest.
Would that you did not go, and yet
It is best, it is best.

Oh! Mister Jesus, you would
Not make your other house like this
It would be sin ......
To make your other house like this.

Oh! how my eyes are wet
And yet ......
This is real hell here
For man to be in ......

The opposite to this
Should be darkness, darkness
Nothing but darkness ......
With not even a bird's voice –

And you, Jesus, there is none of you
It would be awful to see man again
After death, even you ...... you.

– 28 –

WHEN I PRAY

Dark peoples
Singing in my veins
Fair peoples
Singing in soft strains.

O when I lift my hand and pray
I bow with blue eyes
Dark hands
Red hair.

My prayer is life.
O mother and child
In the end
O mother and child.

HOLY

Holy be the white head of a Negro.
Sacred be the black flax of a black child.
Holy be
The golden down
That will stream in the waves of the winds
And will thin like dispersing cloud.
Holy be
Heads of Chinese hair
Sea calm, sea impersonal,
Deep flowering of the mellow and traditional.
Heads of peoples fair
Bright, shimmering from the riches of their species;
Heads of Indians
With feelings of distance and space and dusk:
Heads of wheaten gold,
Heads of peoples dark
So strong, so original:
All of the earth and the sun!

1941

O Solomon's fair
O shadowed flower!

Not black......
Blue sky in face
Strewn cloud
Pollen on cheek
Alack, alack
Not proud
O love their own.

O woven of the night
This beauty of her race
O garden is her hair;
Dawnlight in her eyes
Forgotten surmise
Adam has sown.

O glorious peak
Procreative power
The woman Eve
Twix dark and light
O Solomon's fair
O shadowed flower!

Your blackness steeps through me
It wets like dew
It comes upon me like a lovely night.
You are not here
Your blackness stays round me like rich perfume.
All space black dew.
Your absence beautiful against my loins
Oh! lovely woman like a velvet night!

MOTHER

I saw a woman naked in a river
She was black and in her arms a babe
I saw the river's glory but deliver
Much less than she gave
The great Earth.
I saw happiness within her eyes,
Now the great surprise
She saw me, and made to hide her glory.
Black mother, cradle of birth!
Around her the waters, around swim her daughters.
Black mother, mother of Earth,
Stronger than old boulders, older than what moulders,
Art thou woman!

The waters leapt around her in a wild confusion
Sent silver spraylets through thick black hair,
Caught up her black breasts, and she with easy motion
Kept up her babe and self with slightest fear.
And now she sings above the river's song,
She sings triumphant and with notes held long
She sings of mighty rivers
She sings of noble givers
And with accents strong
She sings of the African womb
Everlasting above the tomb
She sings of her island Jamaica
She sings of the glory of Africa.

With magnificent action of a soul that's pure
As if to pour all riches on a world that's poor
She laughs and makes to show her glory.

I saw her naked
I felt her sacred
She flung back her head and sung her story
Black mother, mother of Earth,
Greater than the mountains, deeper than the fountains
Art thou woman!

New-world Flowers
Spring-time Negroes
The land calling
Clean fresh showers
Of rain falling.
The Grecian heroes
Even features;
These new creatures
With strong noses
Life exuberant
Mouths protuberant
Walking about the world today.

I love Spring-time
I love flowers
I love the freshness of the grass
One day I came upon a glass
Of Grecian make
I would not break.

Classical glass
Far back in thought:
Define our needs
Look what I bought
A pack of seeds
To sprinkle all the world today.

MARKET WOMEN

These people with their golden fruit
Their black hands offer golden suns;
The breeding land it breeds their roots
In mountains, valleys, river-runs
Sun oranges
Bright tropic days:
These people with their scarlet heads
Bear baskets of their golden fruit
Down blue streets
Into market beds
Of leaf green heaps
And crimson blaze,
They stoop before their golden fruit.

ME AN' ME GAL
(Dialect Poem 1933)

Me bus into the city into dis ya town
Me an' me bag me shut pan an' me gal so brown
Lis'en ya wife here we mus' have we chile
In a dis ya gran' place in a dis ya town.
All the city shinin wid de 'lectric light.
All de white man magic mek day from night.
Lawd O! Lawd me Gad yuh great
All men dem a trabil here fus rate.
Like yah 'usband watch black gal a w'ine
In silks an' gran' hats an' shoes so fine
Watch dem w'ine dem backside walking
Down de street, sih yah wha' talking
Dem a put pon whe?

Lawd O siyah God de groun it bun me foot
De road dem is lebel but dem hot me foot.
Me a walk thru' city an' me ha' fe dance
Dis blinkin' hot road mek me more dan prance.
Motor car come shinin' at mos' fas' rate
Lick me 'gainst brickwall, almost bruk me pate.
Hell yah! white man in a four foot sintin'
Man shut in a box say 'im a sing.
See yah wife dis yah whurl is great
Me wi stay yah, suh, wait me fate.
Policeman come, move on son a bitch.
Permanent! man clap me cross wi' switch.
Put me in 'aspital nu'ss dem so kine
See lot 'lectric t'ings see false teeth false eye.

    Walking do'n broad street wid cris-cross light
    Glass shop windah gi' us lovely sight.
    Naygur man in bow tie
    In shoes an' socks

Naygur hooman glide by
With polish locks.

A wait yah, Jesus, a whe she, raise dat head
A naygur hair stay so pon' 'ar head?
See ya wife hurry up wi' dah chile
Losing edication all dis while
Gwine to mek 'im lawyah
Gwine to mek 'im talk suh
Gwine to mek 'im handle
De four wheel ting,
Gwine to mek 'im larned
Gwine to mek 'im fool man
Gwine to mek 'im shine suh before gal.

Some'n come like t'undah a wipe me off me foot
Gran t'ing pon 'undred foot dem call train.
Go do'n tunnel come up t'other side, see 'im!
Oh mek me under'tan' dem ting wi' disyah brain.
Dem 'av patch wuk wire cross ole city
Lady miles away says: "Can't come what a pity!"
Yuh want see man a wheel stick in disyah town
Wan'na see shim-sham, black gal shim-sham.
Wan'na see black boys dress's up in dem tam.
See two storey mam-ma big like jam.

De fus day me come yah me go in a chuch
The chuch gran' so till me nebbah see none such.
De parson an' de angels dress in parrot clothes
Tarapple face man an' 'ooman, sing pray an' pose
White man come, move me out mah seat
Say me dear blackman, use yuh feet.
See from street parson gnash 'im teeth
One more subscriber out a street.

See yuh wife 'urry up ya quick
Gwin' to edicate 'im

Gwin' to mek 'im gran.
Gwin to mek 'im
Lawd mastah
In disyah lan'.
Wan'na see de court house
Wan'na see fight
Wan'na see Naygur
Stan' fe 'im right
Tidder day me look on man
Man lick me wid a brick
Saw de lawd an' Abzra'am
An' Moses wid a brick.

IV

A lovely funeral to the sea
The same for prose and poetry
Only a God alone can see
Through all this green geometry
That pales with days,
For some, grows golden ripe,
For others quick and green,
The philosophy behind a pipe
The waistcoat round a heart
The woman's arms around a man;
The synthesis that forms a part
Of a gold plan
Do what you can
Make all your papers clear
And have no fear
It's a lovely funeral down a stair

Look at Judas, look at me
Two lovely funerals to the sea.

Ancient.
>   These walking wombs
>   They negative what's positive
>   They order tombs
>   For negative and talkative
>   And sadly weep
>   And finally themselves asleep
>   Their kin to weep.

Modern.
>   What do you mean?

Ancient.
>   Developing rooms
>   For living films
>   Out of their wombs
>   Come moving limbs
>   For death to reap.

Blue dew from heaven
Moves through what's given
Of Time in theorems:
This may be nonsense
Few men make sense
On the outside
Of the inside.

INFINITY

Music pure and fine
Two thin cacti leaves
Bend in the air
Leaf within leaf
Note within note
Line within line
I am like a leaf within a leaf
I am like a note within a note
I am like a line within a line
Pure and fine.

HYMN TO BEING

Head to the sky in blue
Roots to the ground in brown
Hands to the world in flames
Freedom the world around
Coffin me not in space
Heaven my starry face
Give me the whole of earth
Wisdom in death in birth.

PASSING

And you pass on and you pass on
A willy-nilly inter-say
We write our hearts
And in our songs
We do not know which day is born
We do not know which life is gone
A willy-nilly all unwise
And in our parts
Of truth and lies
We all move on.

TOMORROW

Tomorrow is an outside world
It moves away from day to day
And leaves me in a futile world
I am the prisoner of my day.
But I can let my fingers touch
The ideal world I cannot clutch
And I can build for other men
Tomorrow I won't know again.

MOUNTAIN PINE TREES

Fine lines the pines
Green light entwines
Old dawning gold;
Which winds are bold
That do not leave
Their hearts to grieve.

Old tents the pines
Green flames the blaze
Where the sun's rose
Knows the wind's ways;
Wild freedom's sigh
The winds blow by.

Soft lines the pines
Sun light entwines;
What singer knows
Which silent hill
What winds are still
What spirits shrieve.

O swirling star,
Pine needles are
Through twisted heaven
Dawn winded, driven;
Star night entwines;
What old wind goes
Which heart is rose?

What form
Of the ghost year
Lingers, and dead?
One who has fled
Comes back with rose tense
Voice like incense
Rising.

It is no other
To my other friend.

It is like the light
Of the walls of my heart
The flowering ruin
Of my stomach
The night and sunshine
Inside shadow.

Is it that I have no body
And you, too, have no body?

It is no other
To my other friend.

— 45 —

A cloud that was the faintest breath
Within a time of gentian blue
And telling more about the sky
Than any dreamer ever knew.

A cloud that was a thing of light
Which any wind would take from sight
Had everything transfigured there
Beyond the sky and everywhere.

A being that was full of grace
Right through the blue and mixed with light
A cloud that would be lost at night.

So sad like the air
Yet the air wears the day
So bright sometimes
In summer days.

So limp like the air
Yet the air bears the night
So full sometimes
In summer light.

Iris – that lasts a day
Springing up in my way.

Angels fair moving by
Bringing you ere you die.

Iris – that lasts a day
Smiling you pass away.

Thou art as gentle as a tree,
In trees no poetry of words
Not any human touch is nigh
The hymns that spread up to the sky.

Thou art as gentle as a tree
And when like trees you look at me
I view you gentle in your way
A tree-like glory to the day.

Oh when the winds that wave your hair
Pass through in music other trees,
Inscribe on winds and cloudy frieze
There was a human angel here.

— 49 —

FOLK POEM

Moon, giddy, newly born
Spilling silver pools of light
Ghost trees for earthly feet.

Play
Moon shine baby
Moon shine baby
Sing out children.

June, giddy, newly born
Shining silver eyes so bright
Spread out in the moon pool;
Moon baby,
Moon baby –
Broken shining plates around her
Gold and blue flakes surround her.

Moon shine baby
Moon shine dolly.

"O stop that" –
Mother cries,
"Mind my baby
Mind my dolly
Mind her eyes!"

June giddy, newly born
Stumbling moonfuls of fright
Now –
Sky dress spread on
Starry pattern

Moon shine baby!
Moon shine dolly!
Merry children.

— 50 —

A LONELY HILL

Full days pass
And a lonely hill
And a single dream
Which way sleep

SMELLS LIKE HELL

The well fed, well clothed, puffing long cigars
In comfort roll down in soft padded cars.
Some men stealing food
To feed their bellies
Women breaking stones
To earn a living.
Well powdered, lip-sticked, smelling sweet for men!
The little beauty
With the peanut brain
She has no duty
That it goes like rain.
Children-bearing women breaking stones
One million children from women breaking stones.
There is no air,
There is no food,
It is hot here
'Twas yesterday
The boss said get out
You are damned rude.

All childless, well slimmed, darling do slim down.
The little beauty
With the peanut brain
She lost four boy friends
But they'll come again.
Some men feeling sick
Can't feed their bellies
What awful boxing last night
The boxers smelled
The nigger in the last fight
Smelled like hell.
All lovely, bath salts, steaming water tap
You're fired, get out, for being without your cap.

What mother, dearest, teach them birth control
A better lesson would be self-control.
Say comrade, listen, there's-no bones to pick
Some must be rich see, some guys must be sick.
The well housed, well served, sleeping in soft beds,
It is hot here
There is no rest
There is no air.

HISTORY MAKERS

I

Women stone breakers
Hammers and rocks
Tired child makers
Haphazard frocks.
Strong thigh
Rigid head
Bent nigh
Hard white piles
Of stone
Under hot sky
In the gully bed.

II

No smiles
No sigh
No moan.

III

Women child bearers
Pregnant frocks
Wilful toil sharers
Destiny shapers
History makers
Hammers and rocks.

In the slums
Jewel staring eyes
Of human flies
Crowd the rims
Of our social order.
We avoid
The stench of slums
Everything uncomfortable
Insistence
Of staring eyes
Evidence
Of substanceless limbs.

Here are –
Bilious houses
At the womb-head
Of comfort
Riches
Pleasure.

Here are –
Magnificent skeletons
With shrinking skins
Shrinking
With our approval.
Here
Here is
The world we accept
From our glass houses.

I sung democracy
And of taking women
They said: no experience.
I said a poet is years older than he is
And knows of women.
I knelt at a flower
And I saw a young bee
Drunken at the flower.
They said adolescence
Write of what you see.
And so I met a woman
A pretty prostitute
Professional:
With feigned surprise
With painted lips
With fixed eyes
With nervy hips.
She held me with artificial touch
The usual touch:
Not even a clever saleswoman
To attitude herself to customers.
And I said what poetry can I get out of this?
And I took me to another brothel
Past a blue light
And I saw a woman
A little white lady
Delicate and white
Resignedly ready
For my body's coming.
And I said can I get any poetry out of this?
And I flit from there
Into the open air
The woman untouched.
And in a side street
A woman brazenly
Offered her body

And I moved away
She following
Even to this day.

And I sounded the seas
And flit to other lands
Into large cities
And on top tall mountains
And into houses
Seeking democracy,
I could not find it as I dreamt it.
Then I raced the world
In some places I found it;
But being challenged, being strangled
Nowhere as I dreamt it.
And I wrote a poem
A phantasy of women
And songs of democracy.
Critical, they said: no experience.

DEMOCRACY

If from this blackness
New flowers shall rise
If out of the darkness
We focus our eyes
Towards a destiny
Towards a nation
Of democracy.
Not now leaderless
With this elation
Work now untireless
Towards this building
Of Socialism.
All our politics
Shall mean much to us
More than the ethics
More than to discuss
What convention is
On a strong axis
Of democracy
Turns our government
Which workers shall know,
Understand, cement
As their property.
This be what we sow
As we dream tonight
That the bricklayers
Agriculturists
Those who control light,
Cleaners, shoe-makers,
Horticulturists,
And devious traders
Help run their country
Part of the great scheme
Of democracy.

ON THIS NIGHT

On this momentous night O God help us.
With faith we now challenge our destiny.
Tonight masses of men will shape, will hope,
Will dream, with us; so many years hang on
Acceptance. Who is that knocking against
The door? Isle of Jamaica is it you
Looking for a destiny, or is it
Noise of the storm?
We want to identify ourselves with
Our people; come close to them and they
Come close to us. People how goeth your
World? Know you with pride in understanding
Or are there hard words in the dark: are you
Formless dust blown in the wind?
Bullets answered your gesture for wages
Sometime back; we give no cause for bullets
We shall lead you to a freedom that will
Elevate you from bullets, shall improve your
Mind: only the stupid stumble in the
Way of bullets.
You are politically dormant; not
Appreciating your democratic
Institutions. Is it not right you should
Know how to use your own weapons of rule?
Let the peasant turn the soil early with the
Dawn and at evening discuss his country
Over his pipe. Let us say our city
Newspapers tell us of abuse and we have peas
To plant tomorrow but our house comes first.
Must the horse rule the rider or the man
The horse.

Wind where cometh the fine technique
Of rule passing through me? My hands wet with
The soil and I knowing my world.

[Written on the occasion of the launching of the People's National Party on September 18, 1938, by N.W. Manley and Sir Stafford Cripps.]

LET US BUILD

Let us build our world firmly brick by brick
Whitemen build
Negroes build
All men build.
Build so
That the world will be too strong for any
Hitlers
And their Aryans;
Too broad for any Ku Klux Klans
Race suppressions
Skin distinctions;
Too united for destroying ideologies
And theologies.
Let us weld
This world so
That men's minds will be too enlightened
To think "nigger"
"Yellow men"
"Can't stop here"
And if our programme means a million years?
What if we must starve and our children starve.
Faith lift our mortal selves beyond tomb stones
We shall build:
Though we die
We shall live!

In promise of electric shocks
With wires naked in death's night
Man's splendid spirit flaming
Assures hills and rocks
Of certain day-light.
We see no wrecked worlds
We see no tombs
But live, uncoffined, flaming.
The globules of these living wombs
If they pass away
My spirit you shall know the splendid day!
But I must marry you
I must bear you there
I must insure you
Survive you everywhere
Under the sweet dew
Over the thirsty land
I hold your hand.
This is the testing
Our tempering.
Spirit, aflame, alive,
Between the fine wedge
Surviving the slicing edge,
Bursting pomegranate pearls
Into the dark night.
Light that will live forever!
Torch that will never
Slip from my hand.

NEW CONSTITUTION, 1945

Now we are tenants at will no longer
There's more room; more right of way
In the land, still not our own,
In the land for us unknown:
And our children; their's to be Home
For tomorrow. Still unpurchased.

Now we turn tenants at will no longer
Spiritual heirs of God. Our spirit stronger.
Let's now look to inheritance
Of our earth. With claim made stronger
By our achievements, our natural dignity.

This land will speak with voices
Of destiny. Voices from victory
Of ownership in proud estate.

SPLENDOUR

Peasant men
Peasant women
Walk sun-wards
Feel certain of your splendour!
Know —
Only gods work the soil.
Longshoremen
Seamen
Love landwards
The land is yours.
Workers
Make glory in your toiling!

Look at us, value us, count us
Today we fight to be free!
Respect us, accept us, know us
Ages you fought to be free!
Your history, your glory, your freedom
Our slavery, our longing, our pining
How dare you defy us, resist us
Today you die to keep free.

TO MEN IN THE INTERNMENT CAMP

Our country is in labour now
For her no rest, no hiding shawl
For her dark aeons woman's thrall.

As many men as scorn her breast
Her sons have known to brave disgrace
Not silent in the market place.

They shine within her eyes firm lights
Deep flowers of her destiny.

Our country is now suffering
Slow is the day of Pain's long night
Our country she shall know her time.
Grass hands for words
Old pasturing;
We, old brothers,
Long nurturing
Our destiny
Our own weaving.

Our country is now labouring
O happy be her flowering!

SING

Sing to me after the elections
Sing to me under the citron trees
Jamaica Jamaicans making
Their Island their country.
Come in every orange breeze
Come to me over the summer hills
Come until your laughter fills,
Jamaica with unity.
Sing to me after the elections
Sing to me under the citron trees
Jamaica Jamaicans making
Their people their country.

CONSTITUTION-DAY POEM

Give us Thy wisdom
More than ever before
Now that our country
Has passed through the door
To wider freedom.

Hold a people's hand
And give us Thy heart.
So that everyman
Lives in the land
And holds dear the part
He must play
To fulfil this day.

Give us Thy Glory
In the days ahead;
O let our country
Be proud of its story
When we are dead!

VI

TOMORROW

Making it music
Making it sleep and turn
Back to daylight
Grass and sky.
Honey evening
Whispering.
Darkness.
Making it sear and burn
Into depths of flesh
Crying
Fretting
Sure of faith;
Despairing
Hoping.
Making it sorrow;
Making it sure then fade
Always a tomorrow,
Always a dream day,
God,
For the labourer.

THE ISLAND

They come to me and tread my soul
They come to me and take their toll
And ever am I brimming full.

But you digging the roads
They rate you as a human bull.
O you burdened with loads
They pass you by, they laugh along,
They steal your ways, your words, your song.

MONEYMAN

O how I hate you, Moneyman.
Your metal hands,
Twin coins in your face,
Your heart clinking
Weaker weaker...
Your soul gushing
Out in dirty filthy notes,
O how I loathe your money talk.

Your brassy contention
For exploitation;
Your metallic argument
Against extinction.

Yet I suppose you are Being also.
I wonder, (you are so minted);
You are the soulless species to us workers;
Even when your voice is soft...
Background: clinking clinking...
Your human touch, your metal squeeze.

But the sun and the moon rise for you also
They rise for the killer and the killed.

The sun for the poet is the kernel rose
The hot flaming fruit of existence.
The face that assumes all that it knows.

You say the sun is the road under your feet
You say the poet thinks the moon is the world,
He is a fool.
You say the sun comes up tomorrow

You say the moon will rise
You say the world goes on
Your cities of metal and pavements go on.

Each day the frantic sun of your world rises;
At night the steel power of your moon
Reflects the artificial lights and the foundries.

And the worker being minted,
The original kernel rose at his back
The immiscible moon paling in fierce cities.

O the worker his eyes peter out to lurid lead.
O horror in tides to war factories
The receding tides to faithless homes.

O how we hate the symbolic stare of your sun,
Moneyman,
The horrid gloss of your moon in dollar cumulus.

O Metalclaw,
O how we loathe you Metalclaw.

Yet know the very truth –
If your sun determines all life, Moneyman,
If you, your sun, your moon, become the influencing system
If men (like me) become the tides pulled back and forth
Your axis will fail, Moneyman,
One day the tides will flood the earth.

GROOVES

He possesses
Pipe and wife
Moving his grooved way
Given
His God and life
Bat-like
In doomed day.

VII

I DREAMED

I dreamed
Jesus kissed Lenin on the lips
For the Russian Revolution.
I dreamed
Jesus walked the streets of Petrograd
Among the workers.
Jesus the perfect man loved and knew Lenin.
He saw the revolution without Him
He saw it with Him
Because Jesus lived a religion
A religion wide as the earth is wide
The religion of Man and Social Justice.
Lenin's religion was
Equality of Man.
The Jesus religion was a pure one
We have distorted
The Lenin religion was a free one
We have feared.

I dreamed
I believe my dream
The lips of Jesus came across the years
And touched Lenin's lips
Lenin anti-Christ
Jesus the earth lover
In love with humanity
As long as the world will last.
I dreamed
My dream is true
Jesus kissed Lenin on the lips
On the lips kissed He Lenin.

MADNESS

They laugh back
Greater lack
So mad man
How they can
Mock divinity
Laugh infinity
Paper flesh
Tinted mesh
More hereafter
Madder laughter
Grimmer dafter
More mad than
Now they can
How mad man.

They who walk demurely
Down cemented ways
Will miss Christ so surely
Christ in modern days.

Workers coming in
Strong and swinging arms
Jesus was in Lenin
With as fierce alarms.

Preachers of religion
Do you know
Christ and Judas were one
More than Christ and John?

My covered stomach I unstomach
My inner self I fortify
A stronger manhood I take on
My very soul I mortify.

The little Jesus hanging by
The little Jesus in a heap
Woman and man in man doth die
The little Jesus fast asleep.

PIONEER

I
When thou wouldst falter
Thou walked on water,
As Christ walked before thee
To Calvary.

II
With failure's halter
Seekest thou water,
In deserts we fear not
Is greenery.

III
The men who would slay thee
With hosannas before thee,
Thou walked on water,
Calm, they forgot.

IV
Now in their chaos
Walk thou like Jesus;
Opening the pod;
Strangely before us,
Always within us,
Bursts forth radiant God.

THE LAST NEGRO

Green flaming wilderness!
White jagged rocks of faith!

The last Negro moves across the world
In his flesh Time's loins
By his side Time's children.

Way back in 1940
There was murder.

Way back
Dawn bent its rose face
Kissed a black animal
Woman of the Negro race
Lovely black animal.

Way back in 1930
There was lynching
He was dangling
And survived his tree.

Spirit in physical
Death is no end of faith!

The last Negro looks into the sun
Into the gold flames
Feeling the heat of stars
And close is God
In creation
In destruction
For Time is God is Man
And peace is chaos.

HARMONY

For our island
Is your continent
And thy countries
Form our instrument:
The strings stretch
From the North pole
To the South pole
And all earth peoples
Live, play, dance, sing
Know the bitterness
In a loosened string
The sabotage of harmony
The utter distress
Of ugly war.

We know one Star
Born from the humblest hearts
The simplest minds of love
And common clay,
Enriched each day.
One world Star
For the peaceful
For the conqueror
For the fool...

For our island
Is thy implement
Your many lands
Our tools of chance.

We make one home
To make merry in
To toil and win

Homes upon homes
Like bees:
World beyond worlds
Of clay and dreams
And rest finally ...

Our island
And thy continent
Be our contentment!

DAWN

Dawn, O strange wild horse
Rushing forth,
Darkness of night in your mane
Wildness of life in your eyes.
Seeker who leapest
Into your dancing song-lights
In all the sorrow of the world:
Dawn is the waves of the sea.
O strange wild Dawn rush on
Over the breadth of the land,
Promise the height of the sun.
Today who lookest down
Thy ways of weary time,
O death will arise from shadows
To-morrow ride forth with thee.
To-morrow come tranquil, Dawn,
Come peace blest.
Dawn, with thy choir-lights
Bring for the seekers flights
     of rest.

VIII

WAR

Isn't it so bright of now
Though cities upon cities fall
And good isn't and good is
That cities are not men at all.

How can woman weep for daughter
Gathered in from the wide world's womb
And man in unnatural slaughter
Scattered back with his hands of doom.

Isn't it so day of night
That fate will pattern on men's feet
And all the falling walls would fall
All failings within street and street.

What does the world ask at its altar
Isn't an altar isn't there none
This man prays for son and daughter
This man leaves to his early son.

MOONLIGHT IN PEACE AND WAR

This garden sunken in moonglow
The peace and beauty long ago.
Away from wireless, sick breath —
All fitful voice of life, death.
This garden sunken in moonlight
And scarcely evidence of night.
Bright mountains heaven's nunneries
In sadder countries fortresses.
The lovely peaks are sky-props
The pines, the flowers moon crops.
Touchless glory at one's feet
Not e'en angel wings shall beat.

World which auctions peace
Man who borrows life
To abuse his time.

Lands which nations claim
Soil which is not ours
To enrich our day.

Mi madre mi padre Tata!

Peace unto peace unto brother
Earth resolve the dead
O earth old mother.

1942

A WORLD AT WAR

They do not know the earth is sick
They sap its strength in unknown excesses;
Perhaps they are right. The earth will return
And gather new life from its deep recesses.

They do not know the earth is Spring
They create deserts, blinding plagues, dumbness;
O that they are right. They will come
Anew, afresh out of old suffering.

They do not know the earth is kind
They catalogue successes and reverses;
O God, they are right? They gamble all –
They make terrible mutual sacrifices.

A TIME FROM WAR

They'll need more than a God to save them now
They'll need more than a universal vow
They must know the terrible truth torn from their flesh.

None of their kind, none as from Nazareth
Not one believing He was all their death
They must feel the powerful re-birth of the earth.

Their God must spring out of their sickened hearts
He must gather oneness from their broken parts
They must turn from their deathful nightmare of their past.

TO KINGDOM COME

I will reconstruct these hills
To Kingdom come.
Death unto life among these heights
And know welcome.
     The hills will tumble and fall
     The stars will slip
     Long midnight over all
I will resurrect from waste till all is done.

IX

EMANCIPATION

Eternal glory to bondsmen who resist their oppressors
O ever pride and full freedom inherit their ancestors.

> The heroes of Emancipation
> Are those who resisted the lash
> The simple spirit and million
> Who resented participation
> In slavery and bond life.
> The heroes the greatest heroes
> Of our country and nation
> Are those who resisted the lash
> And died for their resistance:
> They are the first heroes
> The immortal heroes
> Of the Jamaican nation.

Know there is no disgrace to be cast into bond life
                                        And hate bondage
Know there is no disgrace to be born into bond life
                                        And seek new life
Man's first great resurrection is out of slavery!

O honour life seeking freedom in death
O honour the physical suicide
Whose spirit ranged earth ends for liberty
In refusing spiritual suicide,
Accepting the unknown freedom of death.

O freedom for those enslaved unto death ,
O peace for untold desperate numbers,
Emancipate forever their status
Remembering their bitter enslavement
Forewarned ever our own dignified life.

In the beginning of murder
Many the baptismal dying
In the inhuman passage:

In the monarchy of murder
Not for some resignation:

Here in Jamaica
Memorial lights in our living,
Revolt every five years
In one hundred and fifty years
Twenty-nine revolts in Annunciation
Of freedom, the Annunciation of the Spirit.

Great is the glory of the great oppressed and unconquered
When every degradation feeds the memory of freedom
And questing death is the final mockery of oppressors.

The proudest roads for any people
Is from slavery to nationhood
The greatest moments of history
For any people is in their dark hour,
Faced with resolution and spirit;
Many such hours are rich inheritance
Many such times are before us.

In the perilous road of human forbearance
Know the real heroes;
Those who circumscribed by circumstance
Challenged their circumstance.

On such proud roads
The physical slaves compelled by the lash
The runaway slaves constrained by the land
The revolts of spirit to Murder's saturnalia.

On such proud roads
The eyes without laughter until tears are past.

Know the real heroes
The unnamed and forgotten;
Know also the names preserved
The friends who were friends
The signs in the dark.

> O Daddy Sharpe
> O Daddy Sharpe
> Is a hero of Jamaica
> Remember his name,
> Like Gandhi,
> Sharpe long before him
> Advocate of non-violence
> Was a hero of Jamaica.
> Said won't work as a slave,
> Said don't work as a slave!
> Kiss the bible and be blessed
> Said he kiss thou and be blessed.

> O Daddy Sharpe
> O Sammy Sharpe
> Martyr for Emancipation
> Is a hero of Jamaica.

On such proud roads
The physical slaves spiritually free.

> O Cudjoe was a leader
> Old Coromantyn brave
> Is a hero of Jamaica.

> When the eastern star touches the moon,
> He said
> When the eastern star leaves the east wing
> Of heaven and reaches the moon side.

> Then we all will be free!

The missionaries said so, sang Cudjoe
Old Daddy Sharpe says so, sang Cudjoe.

O Cudjoe brave
O Coromantyn

The east star rides by the moon side

We are not slaves!

On such proud roads
The greater travail in bitter transition
Dumb is delay to the spirit's pre-lived transformation;
Weight of the yoke still felt enlivens suspicion.

On such proud roads
The houses of oppressors pass in flames
The hiding bondsmen ferreted out and killed
The mocking drama of unconquerable bondsmen willed
On their proud roads.

Remember the name of William Knibb
And the old missionaries
From the land of the oppressors
Not only in Christ name did they give
For only in widest freedom men should live.

The clock of freedom now strikes twelve
Knibb said,
The monster is dying, the monster is dead!

On such proud roads
Men who wore their freedom with their chains
Turned dignified, wholesome from their pains.

In perpetuation of Emancipation
Remember the years of struggle:
For perpetuation of freedom

Glorify the martyrdoms
And the crowning August days
Of resurrection and Emancipation:

For the old roads
Lead to new ones
And our fathers are our sons
And our sons are our fathers.
No part of our past that is not
Part of our memory
No death in our past
That is not resurrection unto us.

No degradation resented by our fathers
That is not glory unto us
No suffering of our ancestors
That is not part of our Emancipation.

For man's freedom is something
Men will themselves, in the past, now and
Forever.

POEMS FROM THE 1981 EDITION

THE ROAD

This road we walk
Must be a good road:
A road of good will,
A road of shared suffering,
And joys in the fruits of our yield.
And faith in our deaths.
A road of tomorrow.

We must carve ourselves
From the confusion of a selfish world,
A road of flashing faith,
And calm good sense.
A road that will glance
Like a miracle
And a logical reason
And a greater faith
And religion, than we have known,
Through all atomic clouds
To a way of life:
Such as a man's way with a woman,
Such as fertile earth with an ear of corn,
Such as truth with reason,
Such as flowering in season,
When a collective people breathes goodwill
Because they mean good and are one at heart.

For these things we pray, and live and die.

New York, 1955

LABOUR LEADER

This peasant labour leader,
Suffered a pomegranate wound
Protesting low wages;
His friends eyed the jewelled wound,
Big cymbal on his stomach,
And they saw it darken
And corrode, as the sun sank low;
And they saw the night stars,
And the fading, dumb gaze of his eyes.
Next day, he was the colour of soil,
His eyes dull gravel,
His stomach silent, stark earth.

But someone said:
Seed will grow here again,
The land is eternal…

1978

WORKER

Why praise him lightly when he turns to die?
Maybe the night is bright, his fiery court;
Maybe the darkness for a night of mourning.
New day: the sun's eternal sport
Watching the earth of life and death sorrow.
Now he is dead. Is there for him tomorrow?
His Earth which claims him for her own
Full knows the lover she has sown.

Measure him? His death is living,
Living for the land which knows no death:
He wears the silken day, the veils of night.
His hands that hungered at your heart a time
Are now the trees and paths, his epitaphs.
The stars can tell with their sphinx eyes
He's Earth, her lover, and surmise.

1962

SO WE WON THE ELECTIONS

So we won the elections,
Threw the past like a mountain
From our backs.

Like lovers we now know relief
Because the act is done
The fruit is won.

Know all living begins in reverse;
Now, believe me, we have to return
To the past for wisdom.

And are the best to do so
For we were the victims of the past
The patient ones, who suffered.

We yearned to understand as the poet says:
A man's way with a woman
Or God's way with a man;

We never understood, really,
The earth's way with life.
Or man's deception of man.

Now, we have to be sentinels:
Our heart blood must be watchful beats.
Never must the past return
With dark slavery,
With precise economical serfdom,
With such colonial classical frustration,
And mystic nonsense of loyalty
And artificial protection.

Let the womb know its life
The man, the security, the love
Protectiveness, release, the earth of the womb,
A man his way of life.

We live not this beautiful love anymore.
For in atomic times,
A woman's lullaby
To her child
Must be:
Be calm, baby mine, be calm.
In atomic times
Sleep, baby mine,
Be happy and calm,
Baby mine.

No greater wisdom is the face of disaster.
Or ever will be.

We live in a hydrogen-cobalt age.
When the Sun, and Moon, and Stars, diminish,
In the burning vision of earthly destruction.
So let us be honest,
And understand our age, our souls, our truths,
For the final time.

This road we walk
Must be a good road:
A road of good will,
A road of shared suffering,
And joys in the fruits of our yield.
And faith in our deaths.
A road of tomorrow.

We must carve ourselves
From the confusion of a selfish world,
A road of flashing faith,
And calm good sense.

A road that will glance
Like a miracle
And a logical reason
And a greater faith
And religion, than we have known,
Through all atomic clouds
To a way of life:
Such as a man's way with a woman,
Such as fertile earth with an ear of corn
Such as truth with reason,
Such as flowering in season
When a collective people breathes good will
Because they mean good and are one at heart.

For these things we pray, and live and die.

BLACK CAT EYES

Black cat eyes
Moon shadow dancing
In the duppy walk.

Between mountain
Bamboo trellis,
Depth's darkness
Drums talk.

Pains of Africa,
Joy songs;
Men stalk
In wounded paths.

No more reality from our
Forebears.

Only this fervid languid
Severance
Of limp moonlight
Mountain bamboo trellis
Darkness gaol night.

1955

IN OUR LAND

In our land
Golden-haired strangers
Shining as suns
Find glory.
We know
We are shining as suns also.
In our land
We will find glory.

TANGERINES LIKE TIGERS' EYES

Tangerines like tigers' eyes
Burning in a tropic space
Mountains surge with velvet paws
Rake the heavens in their place.
Hills are fleeced like golden lambs,
Rivers gleam from midnight pause
Crawl a vivid serpent way
Out of darkness into day.
Man awakes with rapt surprise,
Tangerines like silken clams
Tangerines like tigers' eyes
Burning in a tropic space.

1948

UNFOUND

So I have moved you,
So has my heart spoken,
Unseen the falling of dew,
Unfound the road open.

And I have travelled far,
Into vague distance,
The polished glass and the stain,
And the mind's acceptance,
Of all loss and all pain,
And the moving forward.

Who is it held a star
And found the light broken?
Untouched the light in the star,
Unknown the waves shoreward.

O WHEN THE SPIRIT LOVES

O when the spirit loves and the body knows not love,
And flesh is the tortured flute pipe eternal
For the woman the spirit has placed out of reach.

O when the flesh is hungry soil for something to grow
For union like the intimacy of rain, for the seed to be planted,
Fiercely, fully, abandonly, for something to bear;
Then, deny not seed to the spirit, not now!
Not now, when I wish to claim thee from all the elements of earth,
When I wish to claim thee against death, against hate, against fear,
To love thee with the freedom of intimacy beyond God, beyond time;
Nothing that can circumscribe, control, restrain, destroy.
But this God of the Spirit, the most fierce God, the heart of love,
The most relentless torturer of the flesh
Has assigned thee to a place far above
My mortal reach, and abandons me in
The vast spaces of passion,
Where this poem is my hope against distress,
My leaven against hunger, my fanatic psalm,
My fight against frustration by a wilful God.
O when the spirit loves and the body knows not love, knows not love.

POEM FOR RACHEL

When one is young,
Loves music sung and played,
Paintings, wood, stone soul spun,
Things fashioned by the sun
That is the one
For whom the truth is clayed.

When one is young
Loves so creatively
The life of God and men,
That is the one
To whom the songs belong.

New York, May 1, 1960

AFTER READING CHINESE POETRY

Some men when they are old
Dream by the garden gate
The young and rash may scold
Never do things too late
I too at the gate am dreaming.

WHO MADE THE POET?

Who made the poet?
We know who made man,
And the cacti and the rivers,
We know who made God.

But who gave the soul nerves
And blood and flesh
Who made this infinite mesh
Of strength, suffering, nerves?

Not image of God
Not image of man.

So near to God
So far from man.

Who made the poet
So like a tree,
Vision of sky,
Mirror of sea;
Eden and Gethsemane,
Who made me?

1960

OH! YOU BUILD A HOUSE

Oh! You build a house as a woman
Builds a child in her time, building
With the inner vision of her eyes
The knowingness of her being, the whole
Of her living, turned inward, creating.

Here you build a cottage in the hills
And raise up trees every leaf of them
As parents build up their children, wilfully

Who would construct the sky?
Do you know how many visions
Of space to fill the view of your vision.
Where are the unseeing hands that would
Lift up one transfiguration of space
That a child would dream?

Yet you build like the builder of space
The weavers of silences, the constructor of hills
With hands of existence, you propose, the light of your way
I would not tell you that, were it not natural,
Else I would turn away mad like a man
From a mirror who sees the sky in his face
And the resolution of horror and peace in his face
Here you build your house in your hills
Reconstructing your silence like a child
Being endlessly born in its mother
Here you construct your space, every forgetfulness
Every picker of silence, every atom of thought,
Here is the reconstruction of peace, now outside one,
But where a man can turn his energies to his
Innermost being to his own infiniteness.

Where are the succession of stars that are
     the glory of one's mind
Where is the space and the time that can be
     the peace that man should know?
Yes it's good that you build your cottage
And the external comforts of home
Tis the same process and reality backward.

The man in his own inner mind, on his own inner road,
On the most communal journey in the world,
The journey through one to the world of men.
Here, creatively, in the depths of silence
Amidst atomic laughter, the forestry of death,
Elusive simplicity of peace
Must a man build finally...
The reconstruction that is rebirth, in motherhood,
The working of a plot of land,
The growing of grass, warm roses and trees
Reconstruction of the hills, mass upon mass
Reconstruction of the sky, space beyond space:
The infinity of peace.

AND THE SUN HATH FOLLOWED ME

And the sun hath followed me:
Even in winter silence
The blood-dark sun of the tropics
Hast followed me, embraced me fiercely
With the penultimate possession
Of the fantastic tropic sun.

Here in New York, I tell thee
I love you
The love is expression of nature
Wherever nature is
With the language of eyes and of touch
Most eloquent the language of touch
And the infinite ecstasy of understanding
In a stolen peace from the
Fierce wild wilderness of the world.

But the sun is of nature too,
The life of nature
And hath followed me.
Will it take me from thee
With the inviolate possession
Of the frantic tropic sun?
Will it draw me back to the region
Where it draws up trees to its sun face,
Sun truth, possessing the earth,
All life, everything?

1958

WHAT FORM

What form
Of the ghost year
Lingers, and dead?
One who has fled
Comes back with rose tense
Voice like incense
Rising.

It is no other
To my other friend.

It is like the light
Of the walls of my heart
The flowering ruin
Of my stomach
The night and sunshine
Inside shadow.

Is it that I have no body
And you, too, have no body?

It is no other
To my other friend.

SEQUENCE OF POEMS IN THE 1981 EDITION

[George Campbell, by Derek Walcott]

On This Night
Let Us Build
Look at Us
To Men in the Internment Camp
Democracy
I Dreamed
Sing
Constitution-Day Poem
Emancipation
The Road (1955)
Labour Leader (1978)
New Constitution, 1945
Worker (1962)
So We Won the Elections
Negro Aroused
I was Negro
Last Queries
New-World Flowers
Smells Like Hell
Moneyman
History Makers
In the Slums
Mother at Bed of Her Dying Son
Mother
Black Cat Eyes (1955)
Me an' Me Gal (Dialect Poem) 1933
Market Women
Holy
O Solomon's Fair
In Our Land
Splendour

When I Pray
Tangerines Like Tigers' Eyes (1948)
Iris – That Lasts a Day
Trees
Above the Sea
I Will Come
We Went Out Into the Moonlight (1938)
Listen, Moon
Your Blackness
Thou Art as Gentle as a Tree
Fashion a Necklace of Words
Meeting You
My Love
Now I Feel
We Have Visited Strange Places
My Bitter Joy
What Form
When We Part
Drought
Unfound
0 When the Spirit Loves
A Time from War
A World at War
World Which Auctions Peace (1942)
Moonlight in Peace and War
War
To Kingdom Come
Harmony
Madness
My Covered Stomach
Release
Both of Us are Dreaming
I Could Kiss this Place
Essential
Poem for Rachel (1960)

Hymn to Being
After Reading Chinese Poetry
So Sad Like the Air
Passing
A Lovely Funeral
I Sung Democracy
The Island
Ancient and Modern
I Have Done Wrong
The Night
Litany
Flaming Directions
In Memory
Magdalene
They Who Walk Demurely
Blue Dew from Heaven
Infinity
A Cloud
Who Made the Poet? (1960)
Grooves
Mountain Pine Trees
A Lonely Hill
Tomorrow
Pioneer
The Last Negro
Oh! You Build a House
And the Sun Hath Followed Me (1958)
Folk Poem
Dawn, O Strange Wild Horse
In Promise of Electric Shocks
What Form

[Biographical Sketch of George Campbell]

BIOGRAPHICAL SKETCH OF GEORGE CAMPBELL

George Campbell was born December 26, 1916, in Colon, Panama, as George Constantine Campbell Boyd. Until age four he lived on and off in the San Blas Islands, Cuna Cuna Indian territory, where his father, a former Jamaican civil servant, was a Panama supervisor. Later he lived for about a year in Cartagena, Colombia, and Costa Rica and then went back to Panama, where his parents were separated but not divorced because of their Catholicism. He was brought to Jamaica at age five by his mother.

He was privately educated and read extensively. Edna Manley, a sculptor-artist and family friend, discovered his poetry. George Campbell's protest poetry, from his late teens on, was released mainly as part of Jamaica's struggle for independence from England. Norman Manley, outstanding Rhodes Scholar, world-famous law-yer, afterwards Prime Minister, termed Campbell "Poet of the Revolution." He often quoted the poet publicly, and ended his last official foreign address (which he could not deliver personally) with Campbell's racial integration poem, "When I Pray," which Manley always felt only William Blake could have written. (Manley's speech was broadcast in Canada where he was to have spoken, and later published by a Toronto University organ, the *Tamarack Review*.)

During the late thirties and forties Campbell was a prominent contributor to *Focus*, a literary publication co-founded with Edna Manley and others, which gave publicity to writers who were to gain international renown, such as the late Roger Mais.

First Poems was collected and published in 1945, with the collabo-ration of the author, by Edna Manley. It was acclaimed in the Caribbean world and in England as a "landmark" – a breakaway from the Victorian conventions of previous West Indian poetry. The influence of the book has long persisted, and should continue according to Langston Hughes who used Campbell's poem "Litany" in *Poetry of the Negro*, published by Doubleday.

Campbell graduated from St. George's College, then a white, American, Jesuit-run school in Kingston. He worked five years for

The Daily Gleaner, the largest West Indian newspaper, then three years for Public Opinion, a liberal publication. Campbell took over from P. M. Sherlock (afterwards Sir Philip Sherlock), first Vice-chancellor of the University College of the West Indies, the editorship of the *Welfare Reporter*, the Jamaican Government organ for social services. During that period Campbell also edited *The Sun*, for the famous Dr. Lauerbach's "Each One Teach One" literacy program, and was co-secretary of the Little Theatre Movement in Jamaica.

He studied in the United States from 1945 to 1948 at the Dramatic Workshop of the New School for Social Research. He worked on technical matters with Irwin Piscator, former head of the German National Theatre, who had fled Hitler. Campbell also studied and worked with the famous Katherine Dunham Company. He was a librettist for Salvador Ley, former head of the Conservatory of Music in Guatemala. Many Campbell poems were set to music by other composers and used in Carnegie Hall for Pan-American Concerts in America, and they were performed in England at the Royal Albert Hall in 1978.

George Campbell was honoured in Guyana as a poet in the first Carifesta, and his well-known poem "Litany" inspired a symbol of the event: a brown hand holding up a golden sun clasped in the hand. All banners, every craft, and even Guyana's special-issue postage stamps used the symbol. In Havana, Cuba, in 1980, Campbell represented Jamaica as one of the forty-four intellectuals (Gramma Cubana Press), judging 600 entries for Premo Casa de las Americas.

Campbell produced one play, entitled *A Play Without Scenery*; he has written a number of unpublished novels; and he is completing a new book of poetry. He worked as a consultant on publications for the Institute of Jamaica in Kingston.

He lived in New York for the last decades of his life. He died in 2002.

CARIBBEAN MODERN CLASSICS

Now in print:

Earl Lovelace, *While Gods Are Falling*
ISBN 9781845231484, pp. 258; £10.99
Introduction: J. Dillon Brown

Una Marson, *Selected Poems*
ISBN 9781845231682, pp. 184; £9.99
Introduction: Alison Donnell

Edgar Mittelholzer, *Corentyne Thunder*
ISBN 9781845231118, pp. 242; £8.99
Introduction: Juanita Cox

Edgar Mittelholzer, *A Morning at the Office*
ISBN 9781845230661, pp.210; £9.99
Introduction: Raymond Ramcharitar

Edgar Mittelholzer, *Shadows Move Among Them*
ISBN 9781845230913, pp. 358; £12.99
Introduction: Rupert Roopnaraine

Edgar Mittelholzer, *The Life and Death of Sylvia*
ISBN 9781845231200, pp. 366; £12.99
Introduction: Juanita Cox

Elma Napier, *A Flying Fish Whispered*
ISBN: 9781845231026; pp. 248; July 2010; £9.99
Introduction: Evelyn O'Callaghan

Orlando Patterson, *The Children of Sisyphus*
ISBN: 9781845231026; pp. 220; January 2012; £9.99
Introduction: Kwame Dawes

Andrew Salkey, *Escape to an Autumn Pavement*
ISBN 9781845230982, pp. 220; £8.99
Introduction: Thomas Glave

Andrew Salkey, *Hurricane*
ISBN 9781845231804, pp. 101, £6.99

Andrew Salkey, *Earthquake*
ISBN 9781845231828, pp. 103, £6.99

Andrew Salkey, *Drought*
ISBN 9781845231835, pp. 121, £6.99

Andrew Salkey, *Riot*
ISBN 9781845231811, pp. 174, £7.99

Denis Williams, *Other Leopards*
ISBN 9781845230678, pp. 216; £8.99
Introduction: Victor Ramraj

Denis Williams, *The Third Temptation*
ISBN 9781845231163, pp. 108; £8.99
Introduction: Victor Ramraj

Imminent:

Roger Mais, *The Hills Were Joyful Together*

V.S. Reid, *New Day*

Orlando Patterson, *An Absence of Ruins*

Titles thereafter include...

O.R. Dathorne, *The Scholar Man*
O.R. Dathorne, *Dumplings in the Soup*
Neville Dawes, *Interim*
Wilson Harris, *The Sleepers of Roraima*
Wilson Harris, *Tumatumari*
Wilson Harris, *Ascent to Omai*
Wilson Harris, *The Age of the Rainmakers*
Marion Patrick Jones, *Panbeat*
Marion Patrick Jones, *Jouvert Morning*
George Lamming, *Water With Berries*
Roger Mais, *Black Lightning*
Edgar Mittelholzer, *Children of Kaywana*
Edgar Mittelholzer, *The Harrowing of Hubertus*
Edgar Mittelholzer, *Kaywana Blood*
Edgar Mittelholzer, *My Bones and My Flute*
Edgar Mittelholzer, *A Swarthy Boy*
Orlando Patterson, *An Absence of Ruins*
V.S. Reid, *The Leopard* (North America only)
Garth St. Omer, *Shades of Grey*
Andrew Salkey, *The Late Emancipation of Jerry Stover*
and more...